MW01173647

In My Father's House

Jeff Crippen

Based on the sermon series by Pastor Jeff Crippen
Christ Reformation Church - Tillamook, Oregon
January-May 2011

Justice Keepers Publishing

Cover design by Jessica Brown
Layout design by Renee Detig and Jessica Brown
Trinity illustration by Jessica Brown

Images used under Pixabay license (pixabay.com/service/terms).
Used by permission.

In My Father's House: God's Redemptive Plan from Genesis to Revelation

Acknowledgements

I want to particularly thank G. K. Beale, professor of New Testament and Biblical Theology at Westminster Theological Seminary. It was in studying his works on biblical theology that I was greatly helped in grasping the big picture of the Bible and tracing it right through from Genesis to Revelation. I would particularly recommend *The Temple and the Church's Mission* [IVP Academic, 2004] and *God Dwells Among Us: Expanding Eden to the Ends of the Earth* [IVP, 2014] as further help in understanding God's purpose of dwelling among His people.

I also want to thank my friend and co-worker Renee who originally conceived of this book and gathered the main points in it from my sermon series *In My Father's House* (still available on Sermon Audio at sermonaudio.com/crc under the sermons series menu). And then many thanks as well to Jessica for applying her graphics design skills in bringing the book to publication.

May the Lord use our efforts in this project to His glory and for the good of His church.

Introduction

> ⁸ And they heard the sound of the LORD God walking in the garden in the cool of the day, and the man and his wife hid themselves from the presence of the LORD God among the trees of the garden. ⁹ But the LORD God called to the man and said to him, "Where are you?" (*Genesis 3:8-9*)

When Lewis and Clark began their westward trek, they were at a great disadvantage, as are all explorers of new territory. They could see only a short distance around them, but they had no map, no satellite image, to relate themselves and their location to the huge scope of land west of the Mississippi. To understand the parts, we must have a picture of the whole. And this is where so many Bible teachers and their hearers go wrong. They focus on one stream, one mountain, one tree, and try to understand them apart from the satellite image.

The Bible is a unity, written by men who were inspired by God's Spirit to write exactly what the Lord desired to tell us. It is not a haphazard chaos of unrelated data tossed together and bound under one cover. It is one book with one big theme developed by all of its parts. To be ignorant then of that major theme is to guarantee that our handling of the parts will go wrong. And we have gone quite wrong in so many cases.

I remember my father saying to me in passing many years ago, "Why don't they (he meant pastors and teachers in the church) just start at the beginning and go right through to the end instead of jumping all over the place?" My father, as much as I can know, was not a Christian. He would have professed to be and I certainly hope that I am wrong, but I never saw Christ in him. And I cannot help but wonder if things might have gone differently in his life if he had been helped to grasp the things I want to show you in this little book.

Just as God used to walk with Adam and Eve in Eden, and just as He came seeking them out *even after they sinned,* so it is the Lord's desire (dare we say His burning desire?) to walk with us. To live with us…*to dwell and tabernacle* with us as the Bible puts it. And it is this divine desire that is playing itself out in the Promise to Abraham, in the arrival of Christ, and in the cross. Here it is, stated in perfect clarity very, very early on in the Bible:

> 11 I will make my dwelling among you, and my soul shall not abhor you.
> 12 And I will walk among you and will be your God, and you shall be my people. *(Leviticus 26:11-12)*

Do you see it? God, our Creator, the Almighty, Eternal, Creator of all that is, *wants to live with us. He wants to know us, and He wants us to know Him.* The thing is amazing, and yet there it is on every page of the Bible.

> In him you also are being built together into a dwelling place for God by the Spirit. *(Ephesians 2:22)*

So, I invite you to come along with me now as we follow this story right through the Bible. Our journey is a survey – it could easily be much longer and more detailed. But our intent here is to help everyone get a grasp on the lay of the entire landscape so that we can all say, "I see it! Yes! I understand!"

God's Eternal Desire

¹¹ I will make my dwelling among you, and my soul shall not abhor you.
¹² And I will walk among you and will be your God, and you shall be my people. (*Leviticus 26:11-12*)

T.E.M.P.L.E.

We will use the TEMPLE acronym to describe and illustrate God's past-present-future redemptive plan for us in the Lord Jesus Christ: Trinity in Eternity Past, Eden and Eviction, Moses, Poetry and Prophets, Lamb, and Eden Excelled.

God's Goal: Restored Eden

The theme of God dwelling among us can be followed through the Bible by considering each successive appearance of the Temple. With each new temple God brings us nearer to the New Heavens and New Earth, and to Himself. The New Creation has already begun:

> Therefore, if anyone is in Christ, he is a new creation. The old has passed away; behold, the new has come. (*2 Corinthians 5:17*)

... but it is not yet fully consummated. In the New Heavens and Earth, Eden (the first temple) will be not only restored, but exceeded in glory. There will never again be a possibility of sin. A new Adam has come, succeeding where the first one failed.

> Thus it is written, "The first man Adam became a living being"; the last Adam became a life-giving spirit. (*2 Corinthians 15:45*)

Tent of Meeting, Temple in Jerusalem

Near, yet far off

Christ the Second Adam

*Dwelling **with** His people*

Christ's Church

*Dwelling **in** His people*

And the veil shall separate for you the Holy Place from the Most Holy. *(Exodus 26:33)*

And the Word became flesh and dwelt among us, and we have seen His glory *(John 1:14)*

Whoever abides in me and I in him, he it is that bears much fruit *(John 15:5)*

From Genesis to Revelation God draws *closer* and *closer* and *closer* to His people until one day we shall see Him face to face.

TEMPLE Timeline

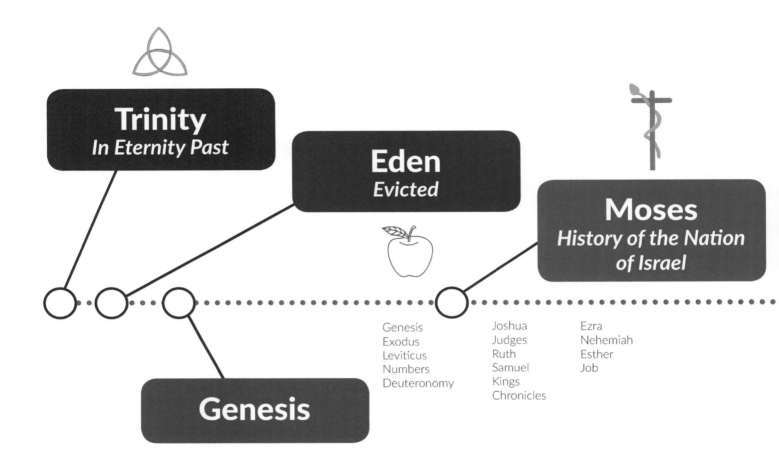

Trinity
In Eternity Past

Eden
Evicted

Moses
History of the Nation of Israel

Genesis

Genesis
Exodus
Leviticus
Numbers
Deuteronomy

Joshua
Judges
Ruth
Samuel
Kings
Chronicles

Ezra
Nehemiah
Esther
Job

Ezekiel   Micah
Daniel   Nahum
Hosea   Habakkuk
Joel   Zephaniah
Amos   Haggai
Obadiah   Zechariah
Jonah   Malachi

Romans   Titus
Corinthians   Philemon
Galatians   Hebrews
Ephesians   James
Philippians   Peter
Colossians   John
Thessalonians Jude
Timothy   Revelation

Poetry and Prophets

Lamb
Christ as the Temple

Eden
Excelled

Matthew
Mark
Luke
John
Acts

Psalms
Proverbs
Ecclesiastes
Song of Solomon
Isaiah
Jeremiah
Lamentations

The Silent Years

Revelation
The New Creation Temple described

TEMPLE

Trinity in Eternity Past

Father

Son   Spirit

God's decree in eternity past is that He, through Jesus Christ and by the Spirit, will TEMPLE with His people.

A Perfect Glory

And now, Father, glorify me in your own presence with the glory that I had with you before the world existed.

John 17:5

A Perfect Love

Father, I desire that they also, whom you have given me, may be with me where I am, to see my glory that you have given me because you loved me before the foundation of the world.

John 17:24

TEMPLE

Eden & Eviction

A temple is a place where God dwells and man meets Him. Of course there are false gods and false temples. But in the Bible we see the living and true God and His true temple.

Genesis 1-3

the first temple

And the LORD God planted a garden in Eden, in the east, and there he put the man whom he had formed. *(Genesis 2:8)*

sin

... just as sin came into the world through one man, and death through sin, and so death spread to all men *(Romans 5:12)*

eviction

He drove out the man, and at the east of the garden of Eden he placed the cherubim and a flaming sword *(Genesis 3:24)*

TE**M**PLE

Moses

The history of the nation of Israel beginning
with Abraham

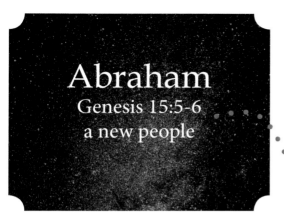

Abraham
Genesis 15:5-6
a new people

5 And He brought him outside and said, 'Look toward heaven, and number the stars, if you are able to number them.' Then He said to him, 'So shall your offspring be.' 6 And he believed the Lord, and He counted it to him as righteousness.

Moses
Exodus 25:8
the tabernacle

And let them make me a sanctuary, that I may dwell in their midst.

Solomon
1 Kings 8:10-11
the temple

10 And when the priests came out of the Holy Place, a cloud filled the house of the Lord, 11 so that the priests could not stand to minister because of the cloud, for the glory of the Lord filled the house of the Lord.

TEM**P**LE

Poetry and Prophets

The language of the Psalms and prophets continues to direct us towards God's ultimate, final, and eternal temple of God: the new heaven and the new earth.

O LORD, who shall sojourn in your tent? Who shall dwell on your holy hill?

Psalm 15:1

The latter glory of this house shall be greater than the former, says the LORD of hosts. And in this place I will give peace, declares the LORD of hosts.

Haggai 2:9

Surely goodness and mercy shall follow me all the days of my life, and I shall dwell in the house of the LORD forever.

Psalm 23:6

Psalm 27:4   Isaiah 51:3   Ezekiel 37:26-28
Psalm 65:3   Isaiah 65:17   Ezekiel 40-48
Psalm 101:4

TEMP**L**E

Lamb

⁶ For to us a child is born, to us a son is given; and the government shall be upon his shoulder, and his name shall be called Wonderful Counselor, Mighty God, Everlasting Father, Prince of Peace. ⁷ **Of the increase of his government and of peace there will be no end,** on the throne of David and over his kingdom, to establish it and to uphold it with justice and with righteousness from this time forth and forevermore. The zeal of the LORD of hosts will do this. *(Isaiah 9:6-7)*

⁹ The true light, which enlightens everyone, was coming into the world. ¹⁰ He was in the world, and the world was made through him, yet the world did not know him. ¹¹ He came to his own, and his own people did not receive him. ¹² But to all who did receive him, who believed in his name, he gave the right to become children of God, ¹³ who were born, not of blood nor of the will of the flesh nor of the will of man, but of God. ¹⁴ **And the Word became flesh and dwelt among us,** and we have seen his glory, glory as of the only Son from the Father, full of grace and truth. *(John 1:9-14)*

When Christ was in this world, come to take our sins upon Himself and to obey God's Law perfectly for us, *He* was the temple. God's plan of dwelling among us took a huge step forward when Jesus was born in Bethlehem. The eternal God had become flesh and dwelt among us.

> 19 Jesus answered them, "Destroy this temple, and in three days I will raise it up." 20 The Jews then said, "It has taken forty-six years to build this temple, and will you raise it up in three days?" 21 But he was speaking about the temple of his body. (*John 2:19-21*)

When Christ ascended into heaven after His resurrection, He sent His Spirit to indwell His true people. This is what the Day of Pentecost was all about:

> 16 But this is what was uttered through the prophet Joel: 17 "'And in the last days it shall be, God declares, that I will pour out my Spirit on all flesh, and your sons and your daughters shall prophesy, and your young men shall see visions, and your old men shall dream dreams; 18 even on my male servants and female servants in those days I will pour out my Spirit, and they shall prophesy. (*Acts 2:16-18*)

Understand? Now *we*, all who are in Christ, born again through faith alone in Christ alone, *are the temple!* Amazing! God is actually in us and the Church is now His temple:

> 19 So then you are no longer strangers and aliens, but you are fellow citizens with the saints and members of the household of God, 20 built on the foundation of the apostles and prophets, Christ Jesus himself being the cornerstone, 21 in whom the whole structure, being joined together, grows into a holy temple in the Lord. 22 In him you also are being built together into a dwelling place for God by the Spirit. (*Ephesians 2:19-22*)

Closer & Closer & Closer
He comes

We are in the Holy of Holies. No more veil of separation.

And behold, the curtain of the
temple was torn in two,
from top to bottom.
(Matthew 27:51)

Let us then with confidence draw
near to the throne of grace, that
we may receive mercy and find
grace to help in time of need.
(Hebrews 4:16)

[11] This was according to the eternal purpose that he has realized in Christ
Jesus our Lord, [12] in whom we have boldness and access with confidence
through our faith in him. [13] So I ask you not to lose heart over what I am
suffering for you, which is your glory. *(Ephesians 3:11-12)*

TEMPLE

Eden Excelled
ETERNAL

When Christ comes again, He is going to radically renovate this old fallen creation and bring to full completion that home He went to prepare for us (see John 14:1-3).

The temple will not exist there in a localized sense, because the entire creation will be the temple, the new Eden. We will be in constant, eternal fellowship with, as John put it, "the Lord God the Almighty, and the Lamb."

²² And I saw no temple in the city, for its temple is the Lord God the Almighty and the Lamb. ²³ And the city has no need of sun or moon to shine on it, for the glory of God gives it light, and its lamp is the Lamb.

(Revelation 21:22-23)

³ And I heard a loud voice from the throne saying, "Behold, **the dwelling place of God is with man.** He will dwell with them, and they will be his people, and God himself will be with them as their God.

⁴ He will wipe away every tear from their eyes, and death shall be no more, neither shall there be mourning, nor crying, nor pain anymore, for the former things have passed away."

(Revelation 21:3-4)

But what about those who refuse to believe this good news we call the gospel of Christ?

Hell

Hell is an actual, real place of punishment
and suffering where many will live apart
from God forever.

Hell is *eternal*

To be separated from God is to be separated from life, from light, from every good thing. God's judgments are ironic. Those who would not have Him and obey and believe Him in this life shall receive exactly what they desired - no God. And that is Hell.

Heaven
the new restored Eden

Heaven is a real, physical place where
believers will live in resurrected bodies
with God, face-to-face, for all eternity.

Heaven is the Christian's eternal HOME

⁴⁰ Just as the weeds are gathered and burned with fire, so will it be at the end of the age. ⁴¹ The Son of Man will send his angels, and they will gather out of his kingdom all causes of sin and all law-breakers, ⁴² and throw them into the fiery furnace. In that place there will be weeping and gnashing of teeth.

⁴³ Then the righteous will shine like the sun in the kingdom of their Father. He who has ears, let him hear. (*Matthew 13:40-43*)

And these will go away into eternal punishment, but the righteous into eternal life.

Matthew 25:46

¹ Then I saw **a new heaven and new earth,** for the first heaven and the first earth had passed away, and the sea was no more. ² And I saw the holy city, new Jerusalem, coming down out of heaven from God, prepared as a bride adorned for her husband. (*Revelation 21:1-2*)

The Narrow Gate

Jesus said to him, "I am the way, and the truth, and the life. No one comes to the Father except through me." *(John 14:6)*

Enter by the narrow gate.

For the gate is narrow and the way is hard that leads to life, and those who find it are few. *(Matthew 7:13-14)*

For the gate is wide and the way is easy that leads to destruction, and those who enter by it are many.

The Sheep and the Goats

[31] When the Son of Man comes in his glory, and all the angels with him, then he will sit on his glorious throne. [32] Before him will be gathered all the nations, and he will separate people one from another as a shepherd separates the sheep from the goats. [33] **And he will place the sheep on his right, but the goats on the left.** [34] Then the King will say to those on his right, "Come, you who are blessed by my Father, inherit the kingdom prepared for you from the foundation of the world ... [41] Then he will say to those on his left, "Depart from me, you cursed, into the eternal fire prepared for the devil and his angels. (*Matthew 25:31-34, 41*)

But nothing unclean will ever enter it, nor anyone who does what is detestable or false, but only those who are written in the Lamb's book of life. (*Revelation 21:27*)

YOU MUST BE BORN AGAIN

[5] Jesus answered, "Truly, truly, I say to you, unless one is born of water and the Spirit, he cannot enter the kingdom of God. [6] That which is born of the flesh is flesh, and that which is born of the Spirit is spirit. *(John 3:5-6)*

[16] For God so loved the world, that he gave his only Son, that whoever believes in him should not perish but have eternal life. [17] For God did not send his Son into the world to condemn the world, but in order that the world might be saved through him. [18] Whoever believes in him is not condemned, but whoever does not believe is condemned already, because he has not believed in the name of the only Son of God. *(John 3:16-18)*

Sermon Titles with Scripture References

In My Father's House
Revelation 21:3-4; John 17

Trinity - Before the World Began
John 17; Job 38

As it Was in the Beginning
Genesis 3; Revelation 21:22-22:5

The Eviction and the Power of Shame
Genesis 3; Romans 5

Call of Abraham - The Creation of a People of God
Genesis 12:1-9; Genesis 13:14-18

Make Me a Sanctuary that I May Dwell in Their Midst
Exodus 25:1-9; Hebrews 9

Near, Yet Far Off
Hebrews 12:18-24; Exodus 40

I Shall Dwell in the House of the Lord Forever
Psalm 27:4-5; Psalm 101:4-8

Eden Expands - Go Into All the World
Genesis 2:7-17; Ezekiel 36:22-38

The Word Became Flesh and Tabernacled Among Us
Hebrews 11:13-16; Exodus 29:45-46

Walking on the Edge - of Hell
Luke 16:19-31; Luke 12:16-21

Everyone Will Be in Their Father's House - The Reality of Hell
Matthew 25:31-46

Which Temple Do You Worship In - Babel or Christ?
Genesis 11:1-9

A Building Not Made With Hands
Isaiah 35; Acts 2:14-21

Raised in Glory
1 Corinthians 15:35; 1 Thessalonians 4:13-5:1

Home at Last
Revelation 21-22

The audio and pdf notes of this sermon series can be found at sermonaudio.com/crc

Recommended Reading

God Dwells Among Us: Expanding Eden to the Ends of the Earth by G.K. Beale and Mitchell Kim

Heaven by Randy Alcorn

The Temple and the Church's Mission: A biblical theology of the dwelling place of God by G.K. Beale